A Code for Living

the Ten Commandments for the 3rd millennium church

Stephen Gaukroger

@Goldhill

THE WORD MADE FRESH!

discussion starters for small groups

A Code for Living: *the Ten Commandments for the 3rd millennium church*

A **scriptureunion@goldhill** product published by Scripture Union, 207–209 Queensway, Bletchley, MK2 2EB, UK. This imprint is especially created to bring the ministry of Gold Hill Baptist Church to a wider audience.

Scripture Union is an international Christian charity working with churches in more than 130 countries providing resources to bring the good news about Jesus Christ to children, young people and families – and to encourage them to develop spiritually through the Bible and prayer. As well as a network of volunteers, staff and associates who run holidays, church-based events and school Christian groups, SU produces a wide range of publications and supports those who use their resources through training programmes.

Email: info@scriptureunion.org.uk Internet: www.scriptureunion.org.uk

Scripture Union Australia
Locked Bag 2, Central Coast Business Centre, NSW 2252 222 Internet: www.su.org.au

Gold Hill: Gold Hill is a Baptist Church and member of the Evangelical Alliance. Their mission statement is: Equipping God's people, Serving God's Son, Reaching God's World. The church meets at Gold Hill Common East, Chalfont St Peter, SL9 9DG. Stephen Gaukroger is the senior pastor.

Email: office@goldhill.org.uk Internet: www.goldhill.org.uk

© Stephen Gaukroger 2004
First published 2004

ISBN 1 84427 041 6

Quotations from the New International Version of the Holy Bible, © 1973, 1978, 1984 by International Bible Society, used by permission of Hodder and Stoughton Limited.

British Library Cataloguing-in-Publication Data: a catalogue record for this book is available from the British Library.

Cover design by aricot vert of Fleet.

Internal design by David Lund Design.

Printed and bound by Ebenezer Baylis, The Trinity Press, Worcester.

Scripture Union: Using the Bible to inspire children, young people and adults to know God

A Code for Living
the Ten Commandments
for the 3rd millennium church
Intro

Amazingly, we are about 3000 years away from the original presentation of what we call the Ten Commandments. It's survived this long because it's been of enormous significance to our society, to our culture, to our church and to ourselves as individuals. At the heart of its significance is the fact that these words are not the words of Moses, the man to whom these rules were delivered – influential though he was – but the words of God himself. God is the creator and shaper of human society and therefore entitled to dictate the ways it's run – its values, rules, guidelines, norms for operating at its best. It's no exaggeration to say that the Ten Commandments have eternal significance rather than merely local relevance.

The Ten Commandments were given in the context of a God who acts decisively in human history (Exodus 20:2). Given to equip the Israelites for their new life, they are firstly **foundational**. They are not of minor intellectual interest, but of major practical importance for the way society operates. Without them, society falls apart. We need a framework in which to relate to each other and if we want the society we have in Britain or in the western world or in the world as a whole *not* to degenerate into anarchy and chaos, we will need to go on reaffirming the value of these commandments as foundational to healthy societal living.

Secondly and sadly, the Ten Commandments are **forgotten**. Polls not just of men and women on the street but of religious leaders reveal that people these days just can't name the Ten Commandments. Most Christians can only get to about six or seven from memory without stuttering to an embarrassed halt. More seriously, they are not just gone from our memory but they're gone from our consciousness. Large numbers of people see no reason why their lives should be bound by them. But God intended that these rules should be functioning, living truth in all our lives.

The Ten Commandments are *not* – repeat *not* – the means of our being put right with God. They are *not* the means of our salvation. People I witness to about the Christian faith nearly always say to me at some point, 'Steve, I'm basically a good person; I live by the Ten Commandments'. The implication is that if I keep the Ten Commandments God will be pleased with me. Of course, the reality is that not a single person has ever kept all Ten Commandments. Neither Christian nor non-Christian can in every way keep their lives in line with them. We can't *totally* put God first in every area, we can't *always* remember the Sabbath to keep it holy, we won't always honour our parents in the way that we're meant to, and so on. And so the Ten Commandments are broken in our society by me, by you, by all of us in some form or other all the time.

But if the purpose of the Ten Commandments is not to make us right with God, the result of them is to drive us in desperation into the arms of a loving God, as we say 'God, I just can't do it!' They persuade us to throw ourselves on God's mercy. We need to be filled with the power of God so that as Jesus lives in us we fulfil the Ten Commandments supernaturally – not by simply gritting our teeth and getting on with it. Because the only way to obey these laws is through a new power and a new heart.

Why not, as a group, read out the Ten Commandments as you begin each meeting with the aim that by the end of the ten sessions you will all have learned them by heart!

Stephen Gaukroger

How to get the best out of **the Word made fresh!**

This series of **the Word made fresh!** discussion starters for small groups provides thought-provoking teaching from Stephen Gaukroger with questions to stimulate discussion and prayer.

The material will suit groups wanting to think about biblical principles as they affect and challenge contemporary life – particularly groups wanting to explore all this within a fairly unstructured programme. It is suitable for newly-formed or established or mixed groups, of about six to 14 members, with limited or extensive Bible knowledge.

It will be helpful if the group leader has had some experience of leading and some understanding of group dynamics, as working with the free format of **the Word made fresh!** will be stretching. Particular attention will need to be paid to involving everyone in the discussion, and avoiding the domination of the conversation by one or two people. It will be a real asset if the group leader has spent time getting to know the members as individuals so that he or she can more readily identify topics which need particularly sensitive handling. That said, the format requires little preparation for the leader apart from a thorough reading of the teaching section and some advance thinking about the questions and Bible verses.

All group members need their own copy of this workbook. Where group members can commit to reading both the Bible passages and the study material in advance of meeting together this can be a real advantage – the group leader need only recall the main points. But if this is not practical, another approach to getting the best out of the material would be to spend 10 to 15 minutes having the study material read aloud by one or more people at the beginning of the session, perhaps in the relaxed setting of coffee and doughnuts.

The worksheet will guide discussion and is intended to be completed during the session. However, the purpose of the time together will be largely fulfilled if the group members have interacted

- with the teaching;
- with the Bible verses;
- with each other in expressing their thoughts and
- with God in prayer.

So completing the worksheet fully or neatly with the 'right' answers is not a criterion for judging the group time! Some people will find it helpful as a record of their thoughts and the discussion, while others will find it a hindrance. Feel free!

A Code for Living
1: Put God first

Exodus 20:3

Here's an email just in. It's from one of Moses' spin doctors.

Dear Moses

Firstly, may I congratulate you on what has been a fantastic campaign so far. The business of the sea opening was very impressive, and the manna provision was social services at its best.

However, it can't have escaped your notice that the party is not wholly behind you. The recent split over the golden calf incident is just one example of dissension in the camp. May I suggest you have become too remote from the grass roots? When you spend most of your time up a mountain talking to a cloud it must be difficult to tune in to the people, but this alienation could be catastrophic. Take your latest initiative – the so-called Ten Commandments. Going up a hill and coming down with a load of laws does not smack to me of democratic government. How can ordinary people be expected to follow laws they have not shaped?

That's why I have set up the Ten Commandments Focus Group. This gives people a chance to comment on the laws and to input the process. The group was designed to be demographically representative of people in the camp; I have been careful to include someone from every tribe. Moses, this is the future of political debate! You must give the people what they want and they will be wholeheartedly behind you. (Until you stop giving them what they want and then they will stab you in the back, of course, but no one said politics was easy!)

Anyway here are the results of the first focus group meeting. Question one was on the number of commandments. 8 said 10 was too many; 3 said 10 was OK; and 1 said 63 would be good because that was how old his mother was. Question 2 was on how the commandments should be drafted. 6 wanted a series of brainstorming meetings; 4 wanted to vote on all divine proposals; and 2 said they were happy for Moses to make suggestions provided they could be changed or ignored completely. Under general comments most of the group said presentation was particularly important. 2 suggested you need a really good video next time; and another suggested the Ten Commandments would be more acceptable if they rhymed.

The Ten Commandments are *not* the product of a democratic discussion. They are revelation from God, a non-negotiable mandate for a healthy society. If we want our children to grow up in a world with good values and standards these laws matter immensely to us. Honour these laws and society will tend to safety, to order, to preservation of its values. Ignore these laws and society will tend to decay and disaster, and it will be under the judgement of God.

Judgement? Where, you may say, is the fire and brimstone? People often think that societies are getting away with disobeying God. God's judgement is only sometimes catastrophic. But it is always continuous. As a society moves further away from God's laws his judgement is progressively released. Society breaks down in direct proportion to its disengagement from commitment to God's values and standards.

The Ten Commandments shout at us across the millennia with a powerful and practical message about right living for our culture. People outside the church think that what the Bible has to say is irrelevant, assuming, for example, that reading about the latest economic situation in the newspaper is totally relevant. Yet if our society was to follow the Ten Commandments there would be a direct impact on every area of life, including the economic. A society committed to the Ten Commandments would need to spend far less money on police and prisons. And, given that so many diseases are directly linked to sin, we would need to spend less on the health service. These are hard economic facts. A society that obeys these standards will save vast sums of money.

Very often our politicians believe they are solving problems when all they are doing is throwing money at some of the symptoms. Much of the behaviour in our society has a kind of self-destruct button. One of the things that frustrates

Much of the behaviour in our society has a kind of self-destruct button

people involved in counselling is that we are forever dealing with issues too late! We are constantly addressing concerns which would not have arisen if only the foundations of people's lives were right. If the foundations of our society are inadequate and weak, it hardly matters what we invest in the superstructure; we have a badly tottering building.

At the time of the issuing of the Ten Commandments, the children of Israel have escaped from the clutches of the evil Pharaoh in Egypt, made their way across the Red Sea and are in the process of forming foundations for the life of their new society. They are little more than a loose collection of warring factions which have not yet been welded into a nation. They are in transition. And they are in need of an underpinning mission statement or a value system – a mechanism which will help them relate to one another. And the Ten Commandments is the societal 'glue' that transforms this bunch of people from being different kinds of tribal groupings into a nation.

What we are witnessing in Britain and many western countries at the moment is the reverse process. We are seeing the decay of a nation into tribal groupings. We are increasingly vulnerable to tribalisation because the glue which has held us together for most of the last century is gradually being picked apart. Therefore the possibilities of civil disobedi-

When we haven't got God
our

ence on our streets, of warfare between different communities and cultures, is increasingly likely. Our common set of standards and values is being eroded, and different sets of morals are being adopted by different groups who come into conflict. Yet the Ten Commandments can provide the foundation on which society needs to be based if it is to avoid descent into tribalism.

In the ancient world there were numbers of gods invented, owned and worshipped by many different groups. The Israelites had just come from Egypt where they had met gods of the Nile and gods of pyramids, for example, not to mention the god who was the Pharaoh. And in their wandering they met many other local deities. But the first commandment they have to understand and live by is that there is only one God – capital 'G'!

Then and now, when *the* God is number one, then everything else falls into place. But when God isn't number one everything else is out of perspective and out of proportion.

In fact, it's remarkably easy for us to get things totally out of proportion in our daily lives. A minor thing can completely throw us into agitation. We lose our focus. We spend whole days worrying about complete trivia. It happens in the local church all the time. People spend hours agonising over programme changes, or something that was said that was unhelpful to them, or the temperature during the service, or the length of the sermon, or the wrong song being sung. Somehow these things can assume enormous significance in our lives. When we haven't got God at number one, our priorities are inappropriate.

This first command radically re-orientates our perspective to what *actually* matters rather than to what *appears* to matter. As well as being important for me as an individual, this is vital in terms of how society governs itself. As

a society abandons God, as God takes less and less of a place, either that society becomes atheistic or it begins to worship a fake god of some kind, and it becomes harder and harder to sustain the moral and ethical glue that keeps it together.

Although philosophers and politicians of the late twentieth century spent a lot of time affirming that you can have a stable society without God, all such experiments are doomed to failure. Unless you have a good and just God, you can't have moral imperatives. All moral frameworks without God are unworkable. Let me explain why: because there's really no reason why we should all adopt the same norms of behaviour as one another unless *God says so*. There needs to be one fixed point, non-negotiable, which no one can argue against. What God says is the only thing that can be right in an objective, unchanging and uncompromising way. So fundamentally the Ten Commandments are right not because they are for the good of society – though they definitely are – but because God himself has determined they are right.

Societies that reject God end up creating their own laws – usually the rules of a dictator, backed by force. But if you want a society that cares for people who are poor and sad and sick, that worries about the elderly and the infirm as well as the new-born or unborn, that treats people with dignity across race and gender and class, then you will not get a better set of presuppositions and values anywhere than the Ten Commandments.

If you want a society which has different values than offered by the Ten Commandments then there will be no moral reason for keeping any rules, apart from the power of the strongest and the brute force of whatever army he can muster to enforce them. You can't have morality without theology. It's difficult to sustain good ethical behaviour without God.

at number one,
priorities are inappropriate

With God as the driver behind these moral imperatives in our society, the church needs to maintain its focus where the first commandment suggests – on God himself. When takes on its right perspective. We need to pray that our community and our world will sense again the value of the framework God has set for the running and ordering of

When God is first in my life, I am changed. When he is first in our society, society is changed

we lose focus on God we argue and fight about things which really don't matter. Most difficulties in church life occur because there isn't a mutual intoxication with the living God, which means we've broken the first commandment.

If you want to know where your focus is in life, then ask yourself what you spend your time on, what you spend your money on, and what you spend your thoughts on most of the time. If your time, money and attention are not directed primarily towards God, you can be fairly sure that the thing that is taking your time, money and attention has become god to you, however much you might protest to the contrary. A fascination with something other than God is a distortion of what's really important. Too many of us are fixated on the wrong things.

As a society we are incredibly absorbed in wanting to fulfil our own selfish desires. I've got missionary friends who, when they come back to this country, wander supermarkets with their mouths open, feeling guilty and disturbed because they can't cope with the choice on offer. Some of us find our whole day is ruined if the size of fizzy drink we want is missing from the shelves and we've only got a dozen alternatives to choose from. Where my friends live in Africa they're thrilled to get *any* kind of soft drink!

We are to model as a church and as individuals that what society needs is an absorption with God – obedience to the first commandment. When we do that, everything else

society. When God is first in my life, I am changed. When he is first in our society, society is changed.

A Code for Living Worksheet

1: Put God first

Exodus 20:3

1 What would you say to the person who argued that the Ten Commandments were only for ancient times and that we've progressed beyond needing them?

_____

_____

_____

2 Why do you think the first commandment begins with God introducing himself (20:2)?

_____

_____

_____

3 Discuss this drafting of the first commandment by Rabbi Chaim Stern: 'I, the Lord, am your God, who inspires you to strive for liberty for all mankind. You shall worship no other gods.'

_____

_____

_____

4 What gods conspire for our attention in today's world?

_____

_____

• How can the church most effectively demonstrate that they are false gods?

_____

_____

5 What instabilities in our society reflect the breaking of the first commandment?

_____

_____

• And what instabilities in the church?

_____

_____

6 'If you want to know where your focus is in life, then ask yourself what you spend your time on, what you spend your money on, and what you spend your thoughts on most of the time.' Spend a few minutes in quiet on your own making a personal priority audit.

• Then share within the group any practical advice you have for maintaining right priorities which allow God to remain pre-eminent.

• Pray with each other for wisdom and vigilance in these areas.

A Code for Living

2: Exclusive rights

Exodus 20:4–6

The first commandment is about worshipping the *right* God. The second commandment is about worshipping the right God *rightly*.

'I am a *jealous* God' we read as part of this commandment (20:5) and this word 'jealous' is unfortunate; it has such negative connotations. Translators have struggled to find the right word. We use it in the context of being envious of each other. But the word is better translated 'zealous'. It is not negative. God is saying that he is zealous, he is very keen indeed, to see his honour established and known. We are not to make an idol because of our jealous or zealous God.

Now 'idol' is another word that gives us problems. It literally means a carving or effigy crafted in word or metal. Even today some societies have household gods – small replicas you can keep on a mantelpiece. Some cultures have huge statues of gods towering over the landscape and visible for miles around.

At this point in the Israelites' history the neighbouring peoples had many gods. Many of the idols, for example, were based on bulls, because the bull stood for strength and sexual prowess. Other idols were based on the female body, representing fertility. But God says that his people are not to use any of these idols or symbols. And neither are his people to represent as idols any of the splendour of his universe. In other words, it was not just that they shouldn't have an idol of a *false* god but they shouldn't have an idol of the *true* God either. Because any idol is bound to be a grotesque misrepresentation of the glory of the living God.

Now the danger is, with our early twenty-first century sophistication, that we can feel certain that we don't have idols. You might be feeling fairly confident that you haven't spent any time shaping or bowing down to a piece of wood or metal recently! So you might be feeling pretty guilt-free in this area.

> You might be feeling fairly confident that you haven't spent any time shaping or bowing down to a piece of wood or metal recently!

We build ever more elaborate shopping malls as temples to materialism everywhere, with piped muzak instead of hymns and the tinkling of tills as an offering

The truth is that the visible idols of the Old Testament have in the New Testament times and down the centuries to today been replaced by idols we cannot see. Though not always visible, they are still idols of our own making; they are still substitutes or cheap imitations we have put in the place of God.

Why do we make idols? Because we ourselves can control them! Look at Isaiah 44:12–20 for biting satirical comment on the folly of the man who is stupid enough to fashion his own idol. How can anything *you* have made be God?

Some of us have made idols of our homes. They are extremely uncomfortable places to visit because the slightest mess is treated with enormous horror – any untidiness means that somehow the idol has been defaced. Many men worship their work – and have made an idol of it to the detriment of God and their family. Some of us have made an idol of our family. Many people tell me proudly that the number one thing in their lives is their family. Often those are the very people who experience disaster in their family life. But where God is first, the family assumes its proper significance.

A car or some other thing that we have bought can become an idol. Or something in the life of the church. There have been periods of church history where the communion bread and wine were so venerated that they were worshipped – making the church guilty of idolatry. Sometimes a physical cross or other artefact or even a place of worship becomes an object of veneration. Any religious symbol has the potential to actually draw us away from God.

There are many idols at the heart of secular society. One of the great idols of the early twenty-first century is the idol of consumption or materialism. Our ancestors bought things in order to survive; they exchanged goods and services and ultimately money came into being as a means of survival. Today shopping is promoted as a leisure activity and we identify ourselves by what we purchase. We build ever more elaborate shopping malls as temples to materialism everywhere, with piped muzak instead of hymns and the tinkling of tills as an offering. We may be defined by what we own, but it's more accurate to say that these possessions own us. Our clothes are not bought to keep us warm but to label us as part of a particular group.

So we have displaced the living God from the throne and have put other gods in his place. Inevitably, we become similar to what we worship – like our idol gods, not like our great God. When the Israelites reach Canaan they find an idol called Moloch who becomes more and more demanding. When offerings of food and animals don't bring rain and victory, offerings of children are required, and then adults. He becomes nastier and nastier and so do the practices of the people who follow him. That's why materialism is such a grotesque corruption. God is not against us having things. He wants us to use things and love people. But what happens is that we love things and use people. There is a resulting emptiness of soul, which materialism cannot fill.

It's time for a spiritual spring clean, when we sweep out the idols and assert our determination to worship God and him only, and not let anything come in the way of that. That process can only begin with a recognition of the problem. Most of us don't want to destroy our idols until disaster strikes. When our marriage fails, or we hear we have a terminal disease, or we are bereaved, or we are rejected by a child, or we're made redundant, or in some other way our world falls apart – then and then only do we recognise there was an idol and come back to God, often in an emotional trauma. We need to understand that idols will always fail us and betray us. Only God satisfies the human soul. There is no substitute. The control we think we have over our idol turns out to be control over us, because the idol dictates our priorities and directs our lifestyle in ways which are ultimately dysfunctional. We need to let God have the exclusive rights to our hearts, which will ultimately fulfil us in ways that no idol can.

A Code for Living Worksheet

2: Exclusive rights

Exodus 20:4–6

1 Why is Genesis 1–3 so important to our understanding of God's exclusive right to be worshipped?

_____

_____

• Give some illustrations of way in which non-Christians you know make idols out of things or people?

_____

_____

• And some ways in which Christians create rivals for God's place in their lives?

_____

_____

• And – for the really brave – describe ways in which you yourself have made idols out of things or people.

_____

_____

2 Take some popular newspapers and magazines and spread them out on the floor or table in front of the group. Can you identify some things that break the second commandment?

_____

_____

• What form does the 'worship' take?

_____

_____

• What is the result?

_____

_____

3 Look at the temptations of Christ in Matthew 4 and Luke 4. Are there any similarities with the temptations we face?

_____

_____

_____

4 Pray in the group for people you know who have made a good thing into an idol, that they will be forced back into the arms of God. (There is no need to name names or give details.)

_____

_____

_____

5 Pray for
• western nations falling prey to tribalism
• for men and women in government to think about foundations and not just symptoms
• for Christians to be salt and light in a broken world

A Code for Living
3: Respect!
Exodus 20:7

At first sight this seems a relatively minor commandment – but actually it lies at the heart of culture decay and decline, and it's a message we need to hear in a country that has largely abandoned wholesale the Judeo-Christian concepts of truth and justice it followed a century ago.

This is one of those verses in Scripture which points quite clearly to consequences. If you abuse God's name, says Exodus 20:7, then God will hold you guilty. In Leviticus 19:12, which comments on this third commandment, we read 'Do not swear falsely by my name and so profane the name of your God'.

Swearing falsely was common in those days. When you asked a salesman, 'Have these goods fallen off the back of a camel?' a common oath of the day would be to raise your hand and swear by God that you were telling the truth and that the goods were excellent and above board. God's name was used to affirm honesty when a lie was being told. The Old Testament makes it very clear that the use of God's name to persuade people that you are telling the truth when you are lying will be met with judgement.

Interestingly enough, Jesus takes this a step further in Matthew 5:33–37 when he talks about how dangerous oaths of any kind are. The Bible is against any kind of casual use of the name of God or any kind of oath.

Swear words come in a number of categories and we're concerned here only with those that use words associated with God himself. This kind of swearing has gone on for centuries. We have in old literature examples of swear words like 'Gadzooks' which comes literally from 'God's hooks' meaning the nails which pierced Jesus. 'Crikey' is a contraction of 'Christ' and 'Blimey' of the curse 'God blind me if what I say isn't true' and so on. But such sayings have become more common in our times and are a key sign of a culture in decay because it's a culture which treats God's name with disrespect. It's a small step from showing disrespect to the name of God to showing disrespect to the person of God.

'Have these goods fallen off the back of a camel?'

Terrifyingly, you can't watch television – even before the nine o'clock watershed – for more than half an hour without God's name being taken in vain half a dozen times. We become so impervious to it, we hardly even notice when it happens. If Jesus is our Lord and Saviour then his name is precious to us and we need to defend that name as the founder of our faith when we hear it abused. Our society is under the judgement of God for breaking the third commandment.

The names of God and Jesus represent authority – and they are the final authority. It's interesting to look in the Bible and reflect on the authority that's invested in the name of God. When we call on his name there's power for salvation, power for repentance, power for revival. Jesus says that where just two or three are gathered *in his name*, he is present to act (Matthew 18:18-20). And the Bible teaches that the name of Jesus is above every name, and it's a name before which everyone will one day bow the knee (Philippians 2:9-11). The whole of Scripture resounds with the names of God and Jesus. It's not simply that we mustn't misuse the names, but that we must affirm them positively. We need to praise the name of Jesus. We must use the name of Jesus in spiritual warfare. We must call on the name of Jesus when we need healing. The truth is that the name of Jesus is still powerful – powerful enough even to raise the dead to life. Peter and John told the crippled man that they had no silver and gold to give him – but they did have the power of the name of Jesus to heal him. It's a high voltage name!

we have the privilege of using the name of Jesus with power

So that's why we should cringe inside when God's name and Jesus' name are blasphemed on our TV screens and on our streets. It's an absolute tragedy that our society has come to see God and Jesus as figures to mock when the truth is that they are the only hope for our world. It's only because God is a God of mercy and grace that those who blaspheme and mock are not struck down. These days there's nothing sacred, nothing beyond the reach of our comedians and satirists. It's twenty-first century cool to push the boundaries. But it's not a trivial matter. My expectation is that these comics will be sad and broken people in years to come. Not that their words can do anything to impair the power of our great God, and not that he needs to respond to defend himself, but that they are greatly diminishing themselves by what they are doing. A society that mocks the name of Jesus will mock the power behind that name and will mock the values behind that name, and this is a process that weakens us all.

Christians are not immune from misusing God's name either. I've lost count of the number of people who have come to me with a good idea and because they want to

we should cringe inside when God's name and Jesus' name are blasphemed on our TV screens and on our streets

convince me about it they attach God's name to it. 'God has told me to tell you …' If that's true, that's wonderful. But if it isn't, may God help you! How dare we affirm our own ideas by dragging God on board! Of course, God does speak directly to us at times and then it's perfectly appropriate to humbly mention that. But the name of Jesus isn't a magic password and shouldn't be used thoughtlessly or for selfish motives. In prayer it's appropriate to use his name in worship or adoration. But it's not appropriate to use it hypnotically like a talisman or lucky charm.

As believers, though, we have the privilege of using the name of Jesus with power. We can call on his name as the one who saves us from our sins (Matthew 1:21), and who can heal our bodies and our troubled minds. We can pray his name over our troubled friends and families, over our troubled communities too. We can ask in the name of Jesus for rescue for problem marriages, for courage to face the worst, for relief from pain. May God forgive our complicity in a nation which mocks his name and values. May we honour the name of the one who has saved us. May we make the name of Jesus great in our worship.

A Code for Living Worksheet

3: Respect!

Exodus 20:7

1 Do names carry much significance in our society?

_____

_____

• Are there names which carry respect?

_____

_____

• Are there names which evoke disrespect?

_____

_____

• What about 'labelling' of individuals or groups?

_____

_____

2 The Black Bible's words for this commandment are: 'You shouldn't dis the Almighty's name, using it in cuss words or rapping with one another. It ain't cool, and payback's a monster.' Why has the concept of 'payback' or judgement such poor credibility in our society and what can we do to change that?

_____

_____

_____

3 What is your personal response when a family member, friend or colleague blasphemes?

_____

_____

• Do circumstances affect your reaction?

_____

_____

4 Can you think of examples in which Christians mis-use the name of God or Jesus?

_____

_____

_____

5 'Blasphemy is the supreme expression of sinful humanity's rebellion against their Creator and rejection of their Saviour. The nation that tolerates it will not survive' (A J Rivers). Do you agree?

_____

_____

• What will it take to turn the tide of blasphemy and irreverent humour in our country?

_____

_____

A Code for Living
4: One day in seven
Exodus 20:8–11

So far we have looked at three very powerful commandments which we know are for the good of our society. We know we should have only one God; we know we shouldn't put anything before that God; and we know we shouldn't misuse the name of God.

But this next commandment is perhaps one of the most difficult to understand in the context of our contemporary world. It's a command that doesn't find any direct support in the pages of the New Testament in the way that the other commands do, and yet it is still as totally relevant to us as when it was written. Implicit in this commandment are significant issues which we face as a society and as individuals for our physical, emotional and spiritual health.

It's clear that the specific feature about the Sabbath as described in the Bible is that it's a day for not working.

There are many reasons for having a Sabbath and clearly not working or resting is the most fundamental. And the slightly ironic comment is added that if God can make the whole world in six days then surely that's enough for you to get all your work done in any given week!

Let's think about the Jewish week and the Jewish Sabbath. The Sabbath allowed time to reflect on significant things other than the routine. We understand that we need special times in the rhythm of our lives when we can focus on things that matter. So anniversaries, for example, are marked and celebrated, and give us opportunity to look

Implicit in this commandment are significant issues which we face as a society and as individuals for our physical, emotional and spiritual health

> As the family gathered around the table they rehearsed together the stories of their faith and the history of God's dealing with them

back and make judgements, and perhaps to look forward and make plans. On the Sabbath the Jews had the opportunity for that kind of reflection every week. After six days of having their noses to the grindstone, working in a mainly agricultural context where the pattern was to labour all the hours of daylight, on the seventh day eternity would invade their time. It was an opportunity to assess where they were, to glimpse the bigger picture.

For the Jews the Sabbath involved rest, worship and family – a healthy paradigm for Christians today. Even when society was in a period of decay, the Sabbath was clearly not used for work (Amos: 8:5). Greedy traders were keen for the Sabbath to be over so that they could get back to the business of making money. The entrepreneurs saw the Sabbath as cramping their style, yet society as a whole was still observing it as a day without work.

If we move on to the New Testament we will see that in the time of Jesus the Sabbath was not simply for an absence of work, but there was an expectation that worship would be a feature of the day (Luke 4:16).

There was also an emphasis on the family. The Sabbath meal, prepared on the Friday evening as the dusk-to-dusk special day began, was essentially a family occasion. As the family gathered around the table they rehearsed together the stories of their faith and the history of God's dealing with them. This was generally not just the nuclear family but included the wider family of relatives of all generations and any friend or guest who was passing through.

Jesus comes into this same context, a good Sabbath-honouring Jew himself, and begins to start to teach people that his followers didn't need to be so tightly bound to the legalistic framework of the Sabbath. He departs from the rabbinic tradition by developing the Sabbath in different ways. So in Mark 2:23-27 there is the fascinating incident of the disciples getting into trouble with the Jewish authorities and Jesus defending them even though on the surface they appear to be breaking Sabbath rules. Jesus says that a new kingdom has come and that the law is now to be interpreted in a different way. The Pharisees observed hundreds of petty regulations that were additions to the law of God, and Jesus cut straight through this, saying that the need of man to eat was more important than ritualistic obedience to a Sabbath principle. The Sabbath, he says, was designed to preserve men and women from themselves; it was created for their use. The principle is for our benefit. In the rhythm of life, if one day in seven isn't a different kind of day we will experience stress and difficulty and cease to be fully functioning as individuals and as a society.

Despite all the evidence to affirm to

that eternity matters –

Of course, the Israelites observed the Sabbath on a Saturday. For the Christians the transfer to a Sunday was in honour of the most significant event in all human history – the raising of Jesus from the dead, which took place on the first day of the week, or Sunday. That single event shocked the early Jewish community to the core. Sunday absorbed many of the characteristics of Saturday and in the early Church those three traditional components – rest, worship and family – were significant, although some were problematic. Slaves, for example, had no choice but to work seven days a week.

So what about us, today? For example, does the Sabbath only mean Sunday? If our commitments mean it's difficult to set aside Sunday as a different kind of day, is it acceptable to celebrate the Sabbath on one of the other six days?

God is not a disciplinarian who wants to make life tough. And yet in our day we have to be careful that the freedom with which we interpret this commandment doesn't mean that legalism has been replaced with licence. If we do this, we rob ourselves of experiencing a special day. At the heart of appreciating the Sabbath are not questions like 'Is it all right to shop on a Sunday?' or 'Can I play sport or watch TV or eat out in a restaurant?' No, behind such questions are bigger issues of what's really important to us.

The passing of laws allowing Sunday trading have in large part made that day very similar to any other, so that within our wider culture the special significance of Sunday has been lost. Christian parents, in particular, may feel great pressure. It used to be that children's activities were all on Saturdays, but now many sports and clubs take place on Sundays. Should Christian parents enforce church and Sunday School or allow their kids to go to football or drama? There's no simple answer. One argument runs that if you force children to church and Sunday School they will rebel in the future. But there are many people for whom that's not true; compulsory attendance has not prevented them from making a Christian commitment. Similarly, there is little substance to the argument that if you allow your kids to go to all these other activities they will be so grateful for your kindness that they will take time later to consider the claims of Christ.

There are no guarantees in raising children. In general I think most parents err on the side of licence. We must remember that the signal we send to our children if we allow them to do other things on Sundays is that church is less important, that the clubs matter more than relationship with God. It is also a sobering thought that we are losing under 15s from church life in frightening numbers. Parents need to work towards helping their children see that Sunday is a day for worship, rest and family – however that is expressed.

Another thing for Christian parents to remember is that having rules about going to church isn't always a bad thing. We operate double standards quite frequently. If you were taking your child to the dentist and the child moaned that they didn't want to go, you're not likely to say, 'Well, that's all right, dear, you don't have to go if you don't want to'. This is because as responsible parents we know that it's good for our children to have regular dental checks otherwise they'll end up with teeth rotting in their heads and you would be seen as bad parents. Not everything that's right to do is easy or comfortable. Despite all the evidence to

the contrary we have to our kids that God matters, and they matter **more** than a football game

the radical disciple of Christ will be determined to strive for a biblical lifestyle even if that means forgoing promotion or employment success at times

the contrary we have to affirm to our kids that God matters, that eternity matters – and they matter more than a football game.

Work commitments are another huge obstacle. Many employers expect that staff will travel on a Sunday to be in the right place for training or work on a Monday, for example. And others are required to work on Sundays to fulfil shift patterns or other needs. However, the radical disciple of Christ will be determined to strive for a biblical lifestyle even if that means forgoing promotion or employment success at times. Over the past two or three decades there have been increasing workplace pressures, demanding more hours and commitment from employees. But our culture is no happier for this concentration of effort, while the prescribing of anti-depressant drugs continues to rise at an alarming rate. In fact, despite improved material gains, studies continue to reveal that we are less happy than in previous decades.

Preachers have always moaned about a lack of observance of the Sabbath. They have concluded – and I agree – that a nation that has given up the Sabbath is a nation that is watering the seeds of decay. We are fighting against the natural rhythm of our lives to our own self-detriment if we refuse to rest one day. We are missing out on developing a vital relationship with God if we refuse to worship one day in seven. How we spend Sunday in detail is not the issue – but the way we spend it needs to be different from the way we spend the other six days. After all, Sunday is resurrection day and we are celebrating that Jesus is alive – and there should be no other place we would rather be than with those who love and know this Jesus! Our Sundays energise us for the other six days. In our Sunday gatherings we sense God's wonderful refreshing touch in our lives individually and together. The break from work allows us to spend time with our families and rest. In short, we spend time recuperating emotionally, mentally and spiritually as we model a radical Christian lifestyle.

Finally, let's remind ourselves that we're only visiting this planet. The six day stuff we do to survive down here on Earth is not the real reason we're here. Our seventh day, devoted to rest, to worship, to the family, is a reminder of the eternal. It's good every seven days to pause long enough to root ourselves in reality and adjust our priorities. As we actively meet with God and let him invade our time and space, he can help us achieve balance and health in all aspects of our life and community. May God help us so to experience the power of the resurrection on Sunday that we can drag that into Monday to Saturday too. We want to be free to enjoy a lifestyle that resonates with God's glory and purpose.

A Code for Living Worksheet

4: One day in seven

Exodus 20:8–11

1 How has the character of Sunday as a special day changed in the lifetimes and experience of group members?

_____

_____

- Do younger members recall stories their parents or grandparents told them about how they spent Sundays? Share your experiences in the group.

_____

_____

2 An old Warwickshire saying is 'Better a man ne'er been born, than he trims his nails on a Sunday morn!' How can a believer avoid legalism at one extreme and license at the other in terms of observing Sunday?

_____

_____

_____

3 Look in Deuteronomy 5:12–15 to discover another reason for observing the Sabbath. What is it?

_____

_____

- Is it important today?

_____

_____

4 The Seven Dwarfs in the children's story sang, 'Hi-ho, hi-ho, it's off to work we go!' A contemporary car bumper sticker has another version: 'I owe, I owe, it's off to work I go!' Discuss the pressures that society's materialism impose on working life.

_____

_____

- How far have you been successful in resisting those pressures?

_____

_____

- How far have you bowed to them?

_____

_____

- Can you share any helpful advice?

_____

_____

5 Does the way you currently spend Sundays feature the three components of rest, worship and family? Is your Sunday unbalanced? Share your reflections in the group and pray for one another for wisdom and courage to re-prioritise where needed.

A Code for Living

5: Now when I was your age...

Exodus 20:12

The fifth commandment is about one thing that we all are! We may not all be married, we are not all old, we are not all parents ... but we are all someone's child.

To a point, no matter how old we are, we remain children; and we have responsibilities to our parents up to and including their deaths. And, if Jewish society is to be understood, that responsibility extends to all the elderly in our society, not just our birth parents.

There are obvious challenges about parenting today which create enormous pressures in society, and the Bible has significant help for this area. This commandment is another key part of the social glue which kept the Israelites together. Jewish society recognised that if you abandon the elderly then you will end up with a cruel and mean society which is increasingly fearful. If in my middle years I see that the way that I am going to be treated when I am old is callously and with disdain, then I am going to be feeling insecure already. And if in my youth I am part of a society that doesn't honour its parents then I am not going to be interested in preparing to be the kind of older person who contributes to society and is respected.

Honour involves three qualities: obedience, respect and care. If you are really going to honour your parents, obedience is vital. Most secular literature about child rearing today emphasises love and compassion but, amazingly, in the Bible parents are never told to love their children. Partly, of course, this is because the expectation would be that you would love your children anyway. But it's also because you can talk about love all you want but unless it has some practical expression it's not real. If as parents we do not

> you can talk about love all you want but unless it has some practical expression it's not real

we feed our children with sufficient food, we clothe them with latest designer outfits, we provide them with the most comprehensive education in history – but their souls are starved

ensure that our children obey us, then we do them a disservice in terms of their relationship with God. Of course, this is probably terribly politically incorrect. But if children can't obey us as their parents, how can we expect them to obey a God they haven't seen? And how can they be expected to obey other figures in authority such as the police and teachers? The Bible's paradigm is that from the earliest days children must be trained to obey their parents. The Bible understands that relationships change as children get older and become adults, so that what is firstly described as obedience becomes respect, then care. In the young child the emphasis is on obedience. But as the child grows and the parent gravitates towards old age, then obedience matures into respect. And then as the parent becomes ill or senile that respect matures into care. If there is never any emphasis on a foundation of obedience then respect will not follow. And if there is no respect, then there is no likelihood of care when it is needed. In that scenario then old people can be abandoned as being nuisances.

We have all kinds of ambitions for our children, many of them very worthy. We want them to excel in sport, to do well in education, to get the great career, to be comfortable materially. None of these are unreasonable expectations. But surely if you are a believer it is not the most important thing. The most important ambition for your children is that they obey God and love him, that their lives are given over to him and that all their lives they follow him. Some Christians are in agony because although their children have grown up to be significant players in industry or medicine or education, they don't know Jesus, and it tears them apart inside.

One observer of British social life has described how at the start of the twenty-first century we feed our children with sufficient food, we clothe them with latest designer outfits, we provide them with the most comprehensive education in history – but their souls are starved, their emotions are hurting and their minds are filled with violence and filth. Our children are not disciplined. We have kept them in ignorance of the laws of their Creator.

So fed up are the police in Texas with dealing with delinquent children at younger and younger ages, that stuck onto the notice board of the police department headquarters in Houston is a list of eight easy rules to make your child into a delinquent. In summary they go like this:

1: Begin in infancy by giving the child everything he wants so that he grows up to believe the world owes him a living.
2: Never give him any spiritual training (that will be propaganda); wait until he is 21 and let him decide for himself.
3: Avoid the use of the word 'wrong'; your child may develop a guilt complex. This way, when he is arrested for stealing a car he will believe that society is against him and he is being persecuted.
4: Pick up everything he leaves lying around and generally do everything for him so he will be experienced in allowing others to take responsibility.
5: Give a child all the money he wants; never let him earn his own (why should he have things as tough as you did?).
6: Take his side against any neighbour, teacher or policeman on the grounds that they are all prejudiced against your child.
7: When he gets into real trouble, apologise yourself. Tell everyone you never could do a thing with him.
8: Prepare for a life of grief; you are likely to have it.

That is from a secular source, produced by people dealing with delinquents and under-age offenders all the time.

If we want to raise a generation to follow the ways of Jesus, we won't necessarily buy into the latest child rearing techniques. Some guidance is very helpful – we mustn't throw it all out – but let's begin with the premise that our babies and young children should **obey** fundamentally. That's not to make us feel good because we become figures of authority, but because if they can't obey us they can't obey God, and then they will not respect or care for the older generation.

– physically, mentally, sexually. That would be utterly against God's laws and values. Proverbs 19:18 clearly links lack of parental discipline with a dissolute lifestyle, a view we find reinforced on the notice board of that police HQ in Texas. If we don't discipline our children and teenagers, we are robbing them of a framework for wholeness.

Many parents refuse to discipline their children on the grounds that they love them. How horrible that Satan has managed to deceive people that discipline is the opposite

We instruct children not so that they make it to Cambridge University or to the top of the corporate ladder, but that they become people who take the faith seriously

Some parents are struggling in this area and need help and are too proud to ask. We feel failures as parents and become insecure and sensitive when the topic of parenting is raised. If we feel we've raised children successfully and can share with others, we need to do it humbly. All children are different. Just because some particular approach worked for your children doesn't mean it will work for children today. If you are a grandparent and you raised children 30 or 40 years ago you need to remember that the world in which teenagers are being raised now is very different. We must help each other and without judgement. If we've failed our children there is forgiveness in Christ. We need not be overwhelmed with our failure but overwhelmed with the love of God and his strength, and his call to invest in the next generation.

Proverbs 13 and 19 have some sound advice about parental responsibility. This includes the controversial advice in Proverbs 13:24 to discipline the child in love by not sparing the rod. It is impossible to use the Bible to defend outlawing corporal punishment for children. The Bible suggests that a smack of some kind is an appropriate part of the disciplinary armour, although the Bible doesn't have the slightest truck with children being abused in any way

of love! Discipline is the *outworking* of love. Deuteronomy 6:5-7 teaches us about instructing children. We instruct children not so that they make it to Cambridge University or to the top of the corporate ladder, but that they become people who take the faith seriously.

Ecclesiastes 12:1 rightly encourages the finding of the Creator in youth. Research suggests that most people who are going to find Jesus in our society find him before they are 20. Let's commit ourselves to assisting that process by ensuring that many children learn godly obedience.

A Code for Living Worksheet

5: Now when I was your age...
Exodus 20:12

1   The Talmud says, 'The honour we give to our parents is like the honour we give to God.' Is this an over-elevated view?

2   Think about the ways in which attitudes towards children and teens and relationships between children and parents have changed in the last few decades. Consider values and identity, family size, education. Share your experiences in the group.

3   Are there qualifications for honouring your parents?

    • What if they are living unbiblical lifestyles?

    • What if they are abusing you in some way?

4   What were your parents' ambitions for you? Were you aware of them? Were they helpful or unhelpful?

5   Why do you think there is a promise given for obedience to this commandment?

6   How is love related to discipline?

7   Rob Parsons writes, 'We are so busy giving our children what we didn't have that we don't have time to give them what we do have.' Do you think this is true?

    • How?

8   Do you personally know some families in crisis or going through particular heartache? Share within the group (carefully keeping confidence where it's appropriate) and finish with a time of prayer for these hurting children and parents.

A Code for Living

6: If looks could kill

Exodus 20:13

Just four little words in English and only two words in Hebrew. Exodus 20:13 is the shortest of the Ten Commandments.

The two simple Hebrew words mean 'You shall not murder'. Now the old translation in English says 'kill', which unfortunately is less specific. The Hebrew means to take someone's life as a vengeful act, as an act of temper, as a capricious, unpremeditated act or as a premeditated, carefully thought-out act of revenge.

Killing was pretty common in the ancient world. Man in his loin cloth took his club and killed animals for food and possibly killed another cave man who was trying to kill the same animal for food. You killed rivals and you killed people who threatened your security. In contrast, we've become pretty squeamish in the early third millennium. In most societies dead bodies are largely hidden from view, whereas centuries ago it was not so uncommon to come across people dying at the side of the road because they were uncared for or because they had been attacked. It's into this kind of barbarous, bloody and violent context that this command is spoken. Life is valuable to me, says the Creator God. It cannot be snuffed out on a whim. This was news to the Israelites.

Which brings us to consider capital punishment. Should a state kill its criminals who murder or perform terrorist acts? In Britain this was carried out in past times by hanging; in America it's by lethal injection or electric chair; other countries pursue more brutal forms of execution. Whether capital punishment is right or wrong is a question on which good Christians have profoundly disagreed and go on disagreeing.

But you cannot argue against capital punishment on the basis of this commandment. It is not a command about society dealing with its criminal element. To use this commandment as an argument for or against capital punishment is using the Bible for a purpose for which it was never intended. But the verse does call us to a commitment to the importance and sanctity of life.

Life is valuable to me, says the Creator God. It cannot be snuffed out on a whim

Let me share a personal view. For many years I have been a member of an international non-Christian organisation which has a concern for political prisoners. They defend people who are in prison for their faith or because of their political views, and I have supported their campaigns. Yet one of the tenets of this organisation is that they are opposed to capital punishment in all forms – while I personally am in favour of capital punishment. I think there are some crimes that are so horrific that the most appropriate response from society is to take the life of the person who committed it. That's my personal view. I am passionate about human rights around the world and feel very strongly about the abuse and the taking of life in butchery and torture and murder by oppressive regimes. But I believe in capital punishment. This command speaks against the casual taking of life, but it doesn't answer the question about whether capital punishment per se is right or wrong. That is an issue we must each come to conclusions about based on other scriptures and with other considerations.

foetus is not really a human life. Clearly this command stands against that. Life is God's gift.

Euthanasia, sometimes euphemistically called mercy killing, is an increasing hotly debated topic. I am not arguing against large doses of pain relief for someone at the close of their life, the unintended consequences of which include a hastening of death. But if we give our doctors permission to become givers of death as well as givers of life we will end up with a much more harsh and cruel society. The sixth commandment comes to us pleading for a softer, gentler, life-sanctifying approach. That's not to deny that there are hard questions to be faced at the beginning and at the end of life. We need to support women lovingly who have had to undergo termination of pregnancy, for example. But the society that treats the unborn and the aged with disdain is a society which will come under the judgement of God.

The womb is the most dangerous place to live in Britain today. Life in the womb has become a disposable commodity

What this commandment says is that you cannot treat life in a cavalier, casual way. In my mind, that means that questions of abortion and euthanasia are actually far more significant than the capital punishment question. In abortion our society is guilty of treating life increasingly casually. The womb is the most dangerous place to live in Britain today. Life in the womb has become a disposable commodity. Abortion is available on demand to get rid of a child because of social convenience or even used as a method of late contraception. Millions of babies have been aborted and continue to be aborted with the excuse that a

The danger is that we all assume we are not guilty of this commandment. If so, we are guilty of pride. Let's look at what Jesus had to say in Matthew 5:21,22. Referring to this command not to murder, Jesus says that anyone who is abusive or angry with his brother will be subject to judgement. Jesus equates the act of murder with a murderous attitude in the heart and mind. Murder itself is the fruit of an attitude. The New Testament take on this is that anyone who hates his brother is a murderer. Hatred is the seed bed of the physical activity of clubbing your neighbour to death.

Which of us hasn't had murderous thoughts? What about when there's a visitor to lunch and the kids play up badly? What about when the baby cries night after night and you can't remember what it's like to have several consecutive hours' sleep? When we're tired, when we're at the end of our tether, something snaps and we feel so angry that love has turned to loathing. We all know these intensely passionate feelings. The only antidote to these murderous feelings is a baptism of love and the transforming power of the Spirit. Not only do we have to resist pulling the trigger but we need to put the knife in its sheath and put the club in the cupboard. That's the only way of fulfilling the sixth commandment.

Not only do we have to resist pulling the trigger but we need to put the knife in its sheath and put the club in the cupboard

Christians need to stand up for the rights of the unborn and the elderly. Murder needs to be opposed in our laws and our values as a nation. But we also need to resist the anger in our own souls that so easily escalates to hatred and murder. And, by the way, not only must we resist the physical act of murder but we must hold back from murdering people's reputations.

May we ask for God's help in honouring life all the way from the womb to the tomb. We need a renewed commitment to the sanctity of life, treasuring the beautiful gift God has given us.

A Code for Living Worksheet

6: If looks could kill
Exodus 20:13

1 'Don't waste nobody' is the stark rendering of this commandment by the Black Bible. Murder is a crime in many countries. But most societies accept that there are circumstances when the taking of a life is necessary or desirable. In which circumstances, if any, do you agree with this?

_____

_____

_____

2 What evidence do you see in society of a change in the traditional view of regarding the right to life as the greatest human freedom?

_____

_____

_____

3 Suicide often speaks of a tragic failure, either of an individual to cope with the pressures of life, or of others to provide adequate support. What comfort would you give grieving relatives?

_____

_____

_____

4 'The womb is the most dangerous place to live in Britain today.' What is your reaction to this view?

_____

_____

_____

5 Generally Christians oppose abortion. Can you think of situations when abortion might be the better option of two agonising alternatives?

_____

_____

• What response should the church make to women who have had abortions?

_____

_____

6 Sir Geraint Archer QC has commented, 'The issue of euthanasia is likely to be the single most important moral issue facing society …' Do you agree?

_____

_____

_____

7 What encouragement on these issues do you find in Isaiah 1:18 and 1 John 1:9?

_____

_____

_____

8 Spend some time praying for those whose roles actively involve them in some of these great moral dilemmas. And for victims of violence.

A Code for Living
7: Marriage matters
Exodus 20:14

Adultery can be defined as the act of fragmenting a marital relationship by a sexual indiscretion or sexual infidelity. It's when one or both marriage partners break the 'one flesh-ness' of that relationship by committing a sex act with someone else.

In the recent past in our country faithfulness in marriage was considered desirable and practised as the norm. But we now live in a society where the small ads in many newspapers and magazines are filled with people openly advertising for adultery. Our culture has travelled far from a commitment to marriage and that's why the church needs to be re-affirming this commandment. The seventh commandment says adultery is wrong primarily because God says so.

Throughout history there have been four ways to get a wife:

- marriage by capture;
- marriage by cash;
- marriage by courtship;
- marriage by consent.

In pre-historic times **marriage by capture** was the norm. You killed your animal and you needed someone to cook it for you and to bear your children, so you looked for an appropriate mate, clubbed her on the head and dragged her by her hair back to your cave.

Then there was **marriage by cash** – a system which still happens in many parts of the world. You, or more usually your parents, would find a woman and debate the price or

> we now live in a society where the small ads in many newspapers or magazines are filled with people openly advertising for adultery

The Bible is angry against adultery because it is sin and has horrific consequences. And at the same time the Bible is incredibly compassionate

the dowry. When the Ten Commandments were written that was the model of marriage which was most prevalent. So adultery was partly wrong in the Old Testament because it was theft. It was theft of the man's property; he or his parents had paid for the wife and she should not be messed with by another man because that would be stealing what was his.

For most of the past century the western world has engaged in a third way: **marriage by courtship**. Couples got together following a series of unwritten but well-recognised rituals, normally concluding with an approach to the woman's father requesting the bride in marriage.

At the start of the third millennium, the common practice is increasingly **marriage by consent**. Little or no account is taken of the extended family; it's just consent between two people. Increasingly no account is taken of the state, in that people are not bothered about whether they get married legally or not. But marriage that's simply the business of two people is a relatively new concept in history. Until this point, marriage has been the responsibility of the tribe or the extended family or the community or the law or the church or some religious institution.

So in Old Testament times adultery was theft of the worst possible kind. Of course, we have moved on and understand that in marriage women don't become the property of men. If men had consulted the first three chapters of the Bible they would see that it is crystal clear that 'for this reason man will leave his father and mother and ... become one flesh' (Genesis 2:24). This is not a model of property owning but of 'one-fleshness' – two coming together as one.

The Bible addresses adultery with two distinct moods. The first mood is anger. The Bible is undoubtedly angry about adultery. God is angry about any fragmentation of a marital relationship. There is holy anger in God's voice, condemning the betrayal of the deepest and most intimate of human relationships. But the second mood is that of compassion. John 8:1-11 recounts the story of the adulterous woman and shows that compassion as exemplified in the ministry of Jesus. The Bible is angry against adultery because it is sin and has horrific consequences. And at the same time the Bible is incredibly compassionate. The Pharisees want to see the woman stoned to death in front of them. On one level they are right, because the law demands this execution. But Jesus sees beyond the mere ritualistic observance of the law. He sees the pain, the anguish and the agony. When God sees adultery he is angry because he sees the sin against his law – but he is compassionate because he sees the damage to human relationships, the devastation in children, the awfulness in the broken home, the guilt and wounds that last for years.

The church has not always got this mood balance right when dealing with sexual sins. Sometimes we have been unbelievably strident in criticising people. People think we are very anti-sex in the church. They think we are prudish, negative and old-fashioned because of the things we say about adultery, about homosexuality, about lesbianism. Of course, we believe those things are wrong. But let's not believe they are wrong out of an attitude of pharisaical judgement, but out of compassion as we see the damage caused in human relationships and society as a whole. Let's be loving and accepting of people even though we are not accepting of the sin. Jesus confronts the sin of the adulterous woman and tells her not to sin any more, but his compassionate attitude allows her to come

We are not treated with respect if we are negative about everything in the style of Disgusted of Tunbridge Wells

to the Saviour. The church tends to drive people away instead of drawing them into the arms of Jesus for forgiveness and cleansing. This commandment is not intended to push people away from God, but to confront sinfulness for what it is. God, with open arms, wants to draw people to himself in repentance and forgiveness.

We do not serve the cause of Christ when others think we are simply against everything. We are not treated with respect if we are negative about everything in the style of Disgusted of Tunbridge Wells. Rather than stressing what we are against we should be affirming the things which we favour. I am in favour of Christian marriage being the model for a safe and secure society. Step by step the differences between marriage and non-marriage, and the differences between heterosexual and homosexual relationships are being eroded. Marriage between one man and one woman is God's standard.

One of the dangers is that we can look at this commandment about adultery and feel an enormous sense of pride and superiority: 'Others may have sinned in this particular way but I have not'. But trust Jesus to bring us back to earth with a bump, because let's look at what he says about our attitude to sexuality. When we looked at the commandment not to murder we saw that Jesus won't even let us get away with hating people. And in Matthew 5:27–30 Jesus says exactly the same thing about adultery.

He says that anyone who looks at a woman lustfully has already committed adultery with her in his heart. And he goes on to describe possible subsequent action in dramatic, violent, abrasive terms.

Now what kind of counselling is that to give to a couple? Imagine going to see your minister or home group leader, sitting in your front room drinking coffee, talking about a marital problem and they say, 'Well, my advice to you is to chop your hand off'. Jesus here is being deliberately shocking, deliberately offensive to human reason. You may not have committed adultery, he says, at least not in the sense of engaging in the coital act. But what is going on in your thoughts has put you on the road towards adultery.

Now the perverse response to that would be to say that if it is just as bad to look with lust as it is to commit adultery, you might as well do it! But, of course, that is not what Jesus had in mind. He is simply making the point that thoughts precede actions. Affairs don't just begin from nothing. When in the office you start to entertain sexual thoughts about the woman who works at the desk near you, that's inappropriate. Those thoughts develop and are sustained. Then there are the chance encounters by the coffee machine and the grabbed lunch to talk about business and so on. It all ends in an affair. But it didn't just happen out of nowhere.

This passage shows us that in terms of psychology and psychiatry, Jesus is a genius. He understands that the eyes are the window to the soul. Now this is a particular, though not exclusive, problem for men. Most men are stimulated sexually through the eyes, while generally women are stimulated through touch. That's why pornography is almost exclusively a male problem. And it's pornographers who are making the real money on the Internet. The Playboy site has something like a quarter of a million hits per day, and that's just one indication of how addicted to sex our world has become. Our teenagers have no concept of a modest society because they have never seen it. Some 80 to 90 per cent of the videos they watch show scantily clad men and women dancing to music while using gestures and actions that are overtly provocative.

The time to avoid adultery is not at the point when you are in the bedroom with someone who is not your husband or wife. That's too late

Sex is used to sell motor cars, ice cream, computers, perfume – anything. Sexuality is aggressively thrown at us in the pages of our newspapers and magazines. Because we are becoming de-sensitised to the sexual agenda, more and more aggressive sexual symbols are used. You cannot flick through the TV channels after nine or ten o'clock at night, particularly if you have cable or digital TV, without seeing images which are going to be unhelpful.

Because this imagery all around us was not available in the past, our thought lives and the purity of our souls is under threat in novel ways in the third millennium. If you want to avoid adultery, you have to start way back here. The time to avoid adultery is not at the point when you are in the bedroom with someone who is not your husband or wife. That's too late. To avoid adultery you start with keeping your thought life pure.

Sometimes I counsel Christians who are heavily into pornography. Their argument is, 'No one else knows, so what difference does it make? It doesn't hurt anyone.' It makes an enormous difference to the purity of your thought life and to the possibility of other temptations to sin. There's no room for arrogance here. It's a good idea to make ourselves accountable to someone else about our thought lives, whether we are married or single. We all need someone who can look us in the eye and ask, 'Is it well with your soul?' There are pressures related to both being married and being single, all of which can be difficult and painful. We need someone who can be close enough to be aware of changes in our behaviour.

Fear is another great motive to be faithful. One of the reasons I am faithful to my wife is because I fear God and his judgement. I fear the consequences of sin and that is entirely biblical.

It's in the interests of society for us all to be working for strong, faithful marriages. If we fail to invest time and emotional energy into our marriages, then adultery is more attractive. If we treat our marriage partners with disdain, then adultery is an option. But if we invest intimacy and freshness into our relationships then adultery is seen exactly for what it is – a horrible and sinister wrecking device from Satan. So let's help people who are struggling in their marriages. Not by wagging our fingers of judgement – but by supporting and caring and doing everything in our power to honour the institution of marriage.

A Code for Living Worksheet

7: Marriage matters
Exodus 20:14

1 Read Ephesians 5:31–33 and discuss what these verses reveal about how God regards marriage.

_____

_____

_____

2 In *The Limits of Sex* Celia Haddon writes, '[one] destructive myth in our lives is that sexual activity is natural, while sexual inactivity is not'. How is this idea reinforced in our culture?

_____

_____

• What can the church do about it?

_____

_____

3 Discuss what you observe of current 'courtship rituals' and what they say about our society.

_____

_____

_____

4 How is sex and marriage talked about in everyday conversation in our society? In our media?

_____

_____

• How can we influence this for good?

_____

_____

5 Is the church meant to be a refuge for the needy and fallen? Or a fortress against them?

_____

_____

• How can the church maintain God's holy standards and yet express the same qualities of grace that Jesus demonstrated?

_____

_____

6 What are the major areas of attack on Christian marriages?

_____

_____

_____

7 Pray in the group for strong Christian marriages that set an attractive standard of excellence for our society; and for a church that will speak out a gospel of forgiveness and restoration for those who have fallen into adultery.

A Code for Living
8: The steal industry

Exodus 20:15

In 2003 the *Reader's Digest* questioned 4000 Europeans about their reactions to a dozen everyday dilemmas to test their honesty.

The Italians were rated as the most honest out of the 19 nationalities, followed by the Finns and the French. Slovakians came bottom of the list, with the Brits well down, in fourteenth place.

- Perhaps unsurprisingly, speeding was the wrong most commonly admitted.
- Seventy per cent of Brits admitted that they would exceed the speed limit given the scenario of a fairly empty motorway.
- Sixty six per cent would jump on a train without a ticket if they were late and knew there was a good chance they wouldn't be caught.
- Sixty five per cent would install an illegal copy of an expensive software programme given by a friend.
- Sixty per cent confessed to helping themselves to stationery or pens from their workplace.
- Almost half of Brits would conceal income on their annual tax return if they thought they could get away with it.
- More than a third would park in a disabled bay at the supermarket if they couldn't find another space.
- One third would queue jump to make sure of a place on a bus and one third thought it was OK to help themselves to nice hotel towels.

- Only seven out of ten would take back £10 extra change to the supermarket cashier.

Generally, women were more honest than men and over 50s more honest than younger people. Of course, this was a self-assessment test. But what do these findings say about contemporary morality?

Try to imagine a world in which every single person was committed to the commandment 'You shall not steal'. You would not need to lock your car or invest in fancy devices

> Almost half of Brits would conceal income on their annual tax return if they thought they could get away with it

The poor were most likely to hand in the wallets with the contents intact while the better off were more likely to pocket the money as an extra bonus

to disable the engine. You wouldn't need security systems and locks in your home. And almost all the goods you bought would be cheaper. If there was no theft, from petty shoplifting through to large-scale fraud of the Inland Revenue, costs for all of us would be significantly reduced.

The society of the Israelites in Old Testament times was absolutely dependent on the commandment 'You shall not steal' being fully worked out in everyday life. It was essential for their stability. When a society is committed not to steal there are enormous ramifications for the happiness and security of the people. If there is no widespread acceptance that stealing is not acceptable, everyday life is accompanied by a great deal of suspicion and cynicism, apart from the extra expense.

There was a huge difference between the way of life of the Israelites and that of their aggressive neighbouring countries. The Israelites lived by God's commandment 'You shall not steal', with the presumption that property belonged to someone else, rather than the presumption that if you couldn't tell who it belonged to then it was yours.

Our culture – and most other cultures – defines theft as the desire to permanently deprive someone of something.

Generally, we have little sense of property as distinct from the person who owns it. In another *Reader's Digest* test, 80 wallets each containing £30 were left in public places around the UK. The poor were most likely to hand in the wallets with the contents intact while the better off were more likely to pocket the money as an extra bonus.

Yet, in the times of Moses, guided by this commandment from God, people understood that property was not available for you to take even it if wasn't physically attached to an individual. If you saw an unattended plough in a field with no one about, you didn't make the presumption that you could take it. Other societies living around the Israelites operated by 'finders keepers'. But God's people made a presumption that the plough did indeed belong to someone, however long they might leave it unattended. The commandment 'You shall not steal' helped the people to maintain the highest standards of personal morality in terms of theft.

Today our relative affluence gives us a different perspective on the implications of theft. If someone steals my TV or my home computer, it will be inconvenient, annoying, and expensive – and dealing with the insurance claim can be time-consuming. But I wouldn't die as a result. Yet in earlier

We are assessed by the car we
the way we dress
Any culture so

times if someone stole your plough or an animal from you, you could well starve to death as a result. Or it might mean great hardship for your children.

In Ephesians 4:28 we see Paul's take on this same command: 'He who has been stealing must steal no longer, but must work, doing something useful with his own hands, that he may have something to share with those in need.' There was a presumption here that you stole because you had a particular need. Interestingly enough, it's only in recent times that stealing has become a kind of leisure pursuit. Most of those who steal in our western societies do not do so out of poverty. Shoplifting is rarely a crime committed by the very poor who need to eat to live; it's a middle-class crime. Paul is clear that the opposite of stealing is generosity and sharing – and that's what we should be about.

But notice what Jesus had to say to the rich young ruler in Matthew 19 – comments which go right to the heart of this command. Jesus is not going to let us get away with the kind of complacency that says, 'I'm OK, I'm not a thief, I'm fulfilling this command.' His reply to the young man that he should sell everything and give to the poor cuts right to the heart of a culture – our materialist culture – whose god is gold and whose creed is greed. Jesus would have understood the findings of the *Reader's Digest* experiment. He knows that the rich are more likely to be dishonest than the poor. It is difficult for the rich person to get to heaven, even if he has kept the letter of the law.

Jesus is saying that in a materialistic culture the state of your heart is absolutely fundamental to this question of theft. Stealing because of poverty is something we can understand. I have been in countries where people feel pressured to steal because their children are starving. I doubt that anyone would want to be overly judgemental of a mother stealing bread for her child. It might still be wrong in some absolute moral sense, and we would want to condemn it. But we would also condemn the culture that made it necessary.

But that's an entirely different thing from what we experience in our culture – a society that is so materialistic, so things-dominated, that it exerts pressures on us to want something for nothing or something that somebody else has. The drive to own and to possess, especially expressed in peer pressure on young people, inevitably leads to a situation where theft continues to happen in alarming and epidemic proportions. We live in a culture which defines the individual by what he owns. We are assessed by the car we drive, the home we live in, the way we dress, the toys we have. Any culture so defined will create pressures to steal. Realistically, some of us are going to have to cut corners if we must access what others have. If we can't achieve possession legitimately then illegitimately will do.

If you look in Titus you'll see that Paul reminds him about this whole business of theft in the context of the workplace. Slaves stealing from their masters was commonplace in the ancient world. Employees stealing from employers is rampant in our culture. This is not a matter of stealing pencils from the office – although that would be included – but it's far deeper and even sinister in terms of our obedience to our company.

It's not just that we are not to steal from our employer but that we are to be fully trustworthy. Christians are called to live every day in the workplace with a higher ethical standard than others around them might display. These are

drive, the home we live in, the toys we have. defined will create pressures to steal complex issues. If we are lazy, if we fail to do a fair day's work, we are in effect stealing from our employer. For many of us who tend to be workaholics this is not an issue, but there will be other challenges. Filling in an expense claim is a challenge to our integrity. Carelessly being late for an appointment means we are stealing someone else's time. Trying to deceive the Inland Revenue is theft, even though it's common sense to pay the minimum amount of tax possible.

If you are a Christian it is vital that you are honest and trust-worthy even in small things. I find that those who strive for honesty in their lifestyle create all sorts of positive witnessing opportunities. One time my parents returned to a supermarket after checking the bill and finding that they

One fascinating aside is that the Old Testament prophet Malachi draws deliberately on this very command in terms of warning about robbing God (Malachi 3:8). A man robbing God is like an ant with a cosh mugging an elephant! Stealing is not just a horizontal interpersonal issue, but an issue between us and God. It is ridiculous that we should dare to try to rob the God of the universe! But that's what happens when your heart is dominated by materialism, the desire to acquire. Not only will you take short cuts with morality; not only will you take things that don't belong to you; not only will you tell what our culture calls 'white lies' or being 'economical with the truth': you will find that you are stealing from God himself because you are not giving him what's rightly his in terms of time, money, energy, talent.

A man robbing God is like an ant with a cosh mugging an elephant!

had been undercharged. The management were baffled; they had not had this situation arise before and didn't know how to deal with it. One day at my local sports centre I was getting a canned drink from a machine when I found a pound coin left behind in the change slot, so I took it to reception. The woman on the desk looked at me as if I was mad! Honesty disarms people tremendously, because it confuses them! And it can be shockingly evangelistic in terms of opportunities.

As believers we are not to be walking around burdened with the slogan 'Thou shalt not steal'. But our whole lives are to be focused on doing the honest and right thing. We will be expressing the generosity that Ephesians says is the very antidote to stealing. Generosity not acquisitiveness will dominate our lives.

What matters most to you? What matters most in our culture is achieving and owning. But if what matters most to you is pleasing God, loving God, loving people; if you've been baptised in the Spirit of God's power and you love the Bible and allow its realities to invade your life, then your priorities will be different.

A Code for Living Worksheet

8: The steal industry

Exodus 20:15

1 Make a list of all the various ways we can 'steal' from others – not just straightforward theft.

_____

_____

• Then list the ways we can 'steal' from God.

_____

_____

• Share and compare with others in the group.

2 Some people think it's OK to steal if the victim is rich enough to afford the loss, or is a big insurance company, or someone who themselves is likely to steal. How has this view become acceptable?

_____

_____

• What's your view?

_____

_____

3 Mark A for 'serious theft', B for 'less serious theft' or C for 'hardly theft really' against this list, and discuss your findings.
   • stealing the reputation of others
   • 'adjusting' tax returns
   • failing to use money for the purpose it was given
   • accepting praise and credit due to other people
   • borrowing time that belongs to God, or the family
   • forgetting to return a loan
   • making a false claim in appealing for funds
   • evading paying a bus or train fare

   • failing to use gifts and resources for the benefit of others
   • not owning up when charged the wrong price

4 How do you feel about:
   • the threat of having your home broken into?
   • the cost of shoplifting that's added to your weekly food bill (likely to be about three pounds a week onto the average shop)?
   • huge numbers of burglaries, thefts and muggings committed to finance drug habits?

5 Are you guilty of assessing people by the things they own?

_____

_____

_____

6 How can an individual have an impact on the tidal wave of thieving in our society?

_____

_____

_____

7 Pray for those who make and enforce laws, those who work in the penal systems, those who work with victims of crime.

A Code for Living
9: Lie detector

Exodus 20:16

Have you noticed how there is a rhythm in the Ten Commandments? They move from the vertical relationship with God through our intimate relationships with one another and then out into the wider society.

The ninth commandment is about the standard of morality we operate in terms of telling the truth and it's expressed in the language of the court. Think of one of those TV courtroom drama scenes when a witness is called to the stand, places their hand on a Bible and says something like 'I swear to tell the truth, the whole truth and nothing but the truth'. The Bible is there as a sign of their commitment to that standard of integrity. Lying is intention to

> Some people have work situations where not telling the truth is part and parcel of everyday life

deceive. A false witness distorts what they have seen or heard or completely invents it. And the Bible says this is wrong. As we live out this principle in a very grey world we will need God's grace and the support of each other in prayer.

Some people have work situations where not telling the truth is part and parcel of everyday life. Some are involved in sales or marketing or some arena of business where distortion of truth is routine. Some who are working at the level of a personal assistant are regularly asked to lie for their bosses: 'Yes, the cheque is in the post!' If that's you, it will be a struggle to live out this command, and there are no simple solutions. Sometimes the whole culture of a workplace demands a level of deceit. In many situations a bending of the truth is expected. As an ex-cabinet minister famously said, there is often a requirement to be 'economical with the truth'.

The Puritans were well known for their commitment to rigorous honesty down to the smallest detail. One leading Puritan proudly boasted that he would never ever tell a

What difference would telling the truth completely and utterly make to your profession? To accountancy? To the legal profession? To marketing? To estate agency?

lie. Two of his fellow Puritans decided to trick him. One went to visit him in his home, and sat down to have a drink with him in his front room. After five or ten minutes, by arrangement, the second friend came and knocked on the door. The Puritan claiming he never lied went to the door. The plan was for the first visitor to climb out of the window while his friend at the door was saying, 'Is brother so and so with you?' The Puritan would, of course, answer yes and then could be accused of lying because he wasn't there any more. But the plan went astray because when he was asked if the man was inside, he replied, 'Well, that's where I left him.' This man certainly had a very strong determination not to be deceived and to tell the truth whatever happens.

Imagine a society now in which everybody told the truth all the time. It would be so much easier to trust someone you were doing business with. What difference would telling the truth completely and utterly make to your profession? To accountancy? To the legal profession? To marketing? To estate agency?

The primary reason for this law is that it flows from the character of a truthful God. There are very few things God cannot do but lying is one of those (John 8:42–44). Not only that, but we learn that the origin of lying is the pit of hell itself. Satan is the father of lies. Of course, lying also comes from our own selfishness. We lie to cover up our own embarrassment or to gain advantage in some way. Or we lie in order to appear better than we actually are. But ultimately the devil is the author and the source of lying. Lying is his native language.

Now most of us are fluent in our native language. We may struggle when we go to Europe on holiday, trying to get by with our school French and a few gestures. But we understand how far that is from being our native language. But the devil lies like a native. He doesn't struggle with it, it comes totally naturally to him. Lying is devilish. It emanates from the pit of hell, and it attacks society.

It is crucial in the raising of children that we help them understand the difference between a lie and the truth. Our children will lie to us from time to time as they are growing up and flexing their muscles; they will lie to get out of trouble, lie to pass the blame, lie to avoid punishment. But we have to help them understand there is a difference between a lie and the truth and that the reason for telling the truth is that truth is from God and lying comes from the devil. If you want to model kingdom values then truth telling will be part of your commitment to becoming more like Jesus, the One who said he was the truth (John 14:6). But without God's power we won't be able to achieve this.

Now some of us have easy settings when it comes to telling the truth. We are surrounded by fellow Christians who love us and affirm us and honesty is not much of a problem. But some of us are in situations in which dishonesty, distortion and the intention to deceive are ever present. That's why we need to pray for each other. Truthfulness will make us stand out for Jesus in a bent world more than anything else.

People ask me about so-called 'white lies' and may claim that these lies don't cause any harm, or even that it's appropriate to tell a white lie from time to time. I want to warn that this concept is extremely dangerous because it justifies something which has its origin in something devilish. Nevertheless, under this heading may come certain lies which are related to social conventions, where there is absolutely no intention to deceive. And also some elements of humour, irony, satire and so on in some absolute sense are lying. But this is not what we are talking about here.

The people who need to feel most challenged by this commandment are those who live a life of situational ethics. They speak the truth in one situation but feel it's acceptable to bend the truth in another. This commandment calls them back to a life of robust truth telling and integrity in every area.

Again, we are not talking about the social convention by which we might answer 'Fine, thank you' when someone asks us, 'How are you today?' You might be really anxious about your job, or have a thumping headache or whatever, but you don't particularly want to share that with the person who' just passing by. So though – strictly speaking – it's lying, there is no intention to deceive; it's a normal part of social interchange. What about when your wife comes home having bought a very expensive dress which she obviously really loves and you hate? Social convention demands

a certain response. Do you opt for rigorous, ruthless honesty? When someone holds up a newborn and encourages you to confess that this is the most beautiful baby in the world, do you hold out for honesty? Most of us think carefully about our responses in these situations and reply either with evasion or with what the other person wants to hear. But this is to do with social convention rather than an attempt at deceit. Because sometimes the truth in these circumstances can be painful.

While most of these are not too serious, we may find we are treading into some ethically ambiguous areas. Think about people who hid Jews in the war from the Nazis. Many people felt that it was OK to lie in the interests of preserving innocent lives. In the early chapters of Joshua a prostitute called Rahab is commended by God and by Joshua for lying to the Jericho authorities. The moral dilemmas are by no means simple. As a pastor I have sometimes had the experience of visiting someone in hospital and being asked by the family not to say that the illness is terminal. In a quiet moment, when the family have gone, and the patient says, 'Steve, is it true that I'm dying?' what should my answer be? I have learned through experience to say that I will not lie but neither will I divulge information unless directly asked.

It is crucial in the raising of children that we help them understand the difference between a lie and the truth

There are times when the choice is not so much between wrong and right as between wrong and worst

So, although it's absolutely right for us to condemn lying and recognise where it comes from, we also need to understand that we are frail people in a fallen world. Also, as Christians, we find ourselves living with many who don't have our presuppositions and values about honesty. There are times when the choice is not so much between wrong and right as between wrong and worst. We must try to make these choices as best we can, with each other's support in prayer. If you buy in to the culture to such an extent that you become comfortable with deceit and distorting the truth, you have misunderstood the Bible. From my counselling experiences I know that there are many difficult and sometimes speedy decisions to face, and there are times when Christians cross the line and make a mistake about truthfulness, and thankfully many have tender consciences and feel pain about their failing. As long as our consciences remain tender in the grey areas there is a chance of us maintaining a lifestyle of integrity.

By the way, some people think that being honest means being downright rude. If you can't express the truth with grace and love, maybe it's better not to express it at all. There's no point in taking pride in speaking the truth if it's causing pain, sadness or anger.

A real encouragement in this area of truth telling is Colossians 3:9,10. Paul says we are not to lie because it's part of the old life we have left behind. Every time you lie you pander to the old life. But we have a new life, we've been born again by the Spirit of God. When we are filled with the Spirit of God, the language of the devil is gone and we speak the language of truth like a native. Until we get to heaven we won't be perfect, but we live with the struggle between the old and new self, the struggle of living in a society or in a place of work where truth isn't valued.

Let's pray for our nation to value the truth and for its people to speak the truth – in the media, in education, in commerce, in local and national government. And for each other that we will have the courage to speak and promote truthfulness in our homes and workplaces.

A Code for Living Worksheet

9: Lie detector

Exodus 20:16

1 How might the breaking of this commandment facilitate the breaking of others?

_____

_____

_____

2 What was the pattern and legacy of lying as described in Genesis 3:1,4,10?

_____

_____

_____

3 Discuss the euphemisms used in everyday speech to cover up lying. What do you think about them?

_____

_____

_____

4 What circumstances do you find most difficult in the area of not responding totally truthfully because of social conventions?

_____

_____

_____

5 Have you ever been a victim of gossip or lies that have damaged your reputation?

_____

_____

• What should your attitude be if this happens to you?

_____

_____

6 How can we encourage young children to tell the truth without suppressing their lively imaginations?

_____

_____

_____

7 Read Colossians 3:5–10. Share any experiences you have had of being released from lying as part of your old life.

_____

_____

_____

8 Share your current struggles in the area of truth telling, whether that's in the workplace or in the home. Pray for one another.

A Code for Living
10: An affair of the heart

Exodus 20:17

While cynics argue that this is the least important commandment, coveting is a deeply ingrained problem of our third millennium society.

In fact, I would say that if we could just obey this one commandment it would have such an impact on our lifestyles that the change would perhaps draw more people to Christ than anything else!

So far the commands have challenged our relationship with God and our relationship with each other and with society. But this is the only command that is not to do with an action but with an attitude. Whereas murder and adultery are more easily defined, this command about covetousness goes behind the activity to the attitude. If we are to fulfil this we need radical heart surgery.

This command also provides a bridge from the Old into the New Testament. Jesus understood all about the importance of not coveting, because in his teaching he continually took people behind the scenes, from the seen to the unseen. He's concerned with our motives. He's interested in what causes us to murder or lie or commit adultery. So he's concerned with our thought lives and attitudes.

By being literal in our interpretation of this commandment, we try to create an escape clause. Some years ago I heard a comedian tell his audience that he wouldn't ever covet his neighbour's wife because she was particularly ugly. Similarly, many people could claim that they've never coveted their neighbour's ox or donkey. But this isn't about wives or oxen or donkeys. These were the appropriate symbols of wealth at that time. What is it for us? If I am a normal twenty-first century male I will want a nice car – the best, the fastest, the most expensive. So what's

Some years ago I heard a comedian tell his audience that he wouldn't ever covet his neighbour's wife because she was particularly ugly

There's constant pressure from seductive advertising, generally featuring gorgeous young women, to buy, buy, buy – because we're worth it!

changed? Have you never coveted another person's sports car? We still covet other people's symbols of wealth. I want all the symbols and attributes of wealth that you have.

So covetousness – the desire to acquire – is potent in our society, and reveals itself in envy. Greed is good in our culture. We make money by encouraging people to want more. That's the basis of capitalist society. Our god is gold and our creed is greed. In Luke 12:13–15 Jesus warns us to be on our guard against greed and says that 'a man's life does not consist in the abundance of his possessions'. That's the complete opposite of the values around me. Jesus goes on to tell the story of a man who had all the possessions he could wish for, but when he died God said he was a fool.

Every day we are bombarded with advertising encouraging us to acquire. There are things that you didn't know you needed until someone told you. There are things that you need to replace because they're not the latest with all the bells and whistles even though your old one's working fine. There's constant pressure from seductive advertising, generally featuring gorgeous young women, to buy, buy, buy – because we're worth it! These past few years we've been persuaded that we need conditioner as well as shampoo, even though over centuries people managed quite happily without it. Now it's an essential requirement of personal hygiene. Advertising persuades us that the choices we make when we shop are what's important in life, that it's absolutely my right to have the best and the latest. What a pathetic, sick society we are! We are encouraged to want and acquire and the process bypasses our brains and our spirits.

In complete contrast, the Bible speaks up for a being satisfied with enough (Philippians 4:12). Today that is radical thinking. If Christians could grasp this properly it would revolutionise our Christian walk.

John Wesley probably earned about £28 a year when he started his preaching ministry and 34 years later he may have been earning £1500 or £1600, but he was still living

on £28 because he understood what enough was. Our society says there is never enough; there is always something else we want tomorrow or the next day. We only feel fulfilled when we go on consuming. The sin of post-modernity is the sin of consumerism. Even worse than being defined by what I own, now I am defined by what I consume and what I go on acquiring. Sadly, many of the very rich discover that all their goods simply haven't bought them happiness.

Ever been hill climbing and looked out when you got to the summit only to see that the next hill is just slightly higher and you feel frustrated and can't enjoy the view because that's where you want to be? Perhaps you have an ambition to be as rich as Bill Gates? Or maybe you think that if you had just a little bit more you'd be happier? But just how many meals can you eat? How many clothes can you wear? How many toys can you collect? We need to ask God to help us see him as enough, and that's the best antidote for the culture of acquisition. Paul says he learned the secret of being content in every and any situation. That's a secret worth learning! He knew what it was to have enough.

So this command is an affair of the heart. We need to ask God to fill us with himself and help us learn that he is enough for us. This process is helped along if we cultivate generosity – giving away what we have. We need to understand that we have no right to the things we call our own – they are all God's. Understanding that releases us to let people into our homes, borrow our cars, use anything that's ours.

Finally, let's remind ourselves of what Jesus called the greatest commandment (Matthew 22:37) – to love God with all your heart, soul and mind and your neighbour as yourself. Every one of the Ten Commandments finds its fulfilment in love for God and love for others. Love fulfils the law, internalising the transformations of radical surgery in my life.

A Code for Living Worksheet

10: An affair of the heart

Exodus 20:17

1   What symbols of achievement or wealth are most coveted in our society?

_____

_____

• Is the church immune, or do we have other symbols?

_____

_____

2   What do you think a covetous heart reveals about our relationship with God?

_____

_____

_____

3   How is a covetous heart revealed in the following verses: Amos 8:4–6; I Kings 21; Jeremiah 7:1–15; 2 Samuel 11–12.

_____

_____

_____

4   Look for antidotes to covetousness in Psalm 16:5; 1 Timothy 6:6-10; Acts 20:35; Hebrews 13:5; Matthew 6:31–33.

_____

_____

• Can you list any others from your own experiences?

_____

_____

5   What kinds of advertising are you most likely to fall prey to?

_____

_____

_____

6   What is the difference between covetousness and ambition?

_____

_____

_____

7   Reflect on the Ten Commandments as a whole. How might the church re-establish their value for third millennium citizens?

_____

_____

_____

8   Pray for the covetousness of our rich society, that we will learn to share generously with nations in need. And pray for each other, to learn more about generosity on a personal level.

the Word made fresh! -

other titles from Stephen Gaukroger

Revival Living

insights from 1 Timothy for the 3rd millennium church

Paul's been there, done that – and got the t-shirt! He's planted churches all over the ancient world – congregations of living, vibrant believers. He's seen miracles and disappointments. He's experienced success and endured the most incredible opposition. Nearing the end of his days, far from being a spent force, he's still passionately full of joy and faith – and still looking for revival.

Is that our longing? Do we want the cobwebs of our mediocrity to be blown away by the breath of God? Take Paul's advice to Timothy on how to live a godly life, how to set an example as a leader, how to communicate a gospel free from error, how to be the best you can for God.

ISBN 1 84427 042 4

Transition Living

insights from 1 Samuel for the 3rd millennium church

From the big picture of international politics and business right through to the daily routines of individuals in our planet's many and varied nations, the current agenda is typically one of massive change – and the climate a loss of confidence and equilibrium. Culturally, many parts of western society face moral decline, and family and community meltdown.

Have we been here before? Are there lessons to learn from the past? The days of Old Testament giants Samuel, Saul and David were similarly unsettled, as the 12 tribes of Israel struggled with the transition to nationhood. There are principles and parallels here to impact us personally and nationally on our faith journeys.

ISBN 1 84427 040 8

Available from Christian bookshops or from Scripture Union Mail Order:
PO Box 5148, Milton Keynes MLO, MK2 2YX, tel 01908 856006 or online through www.scriptureunion.org.uk